Throw a Tomato

and 151 other ways to be mean and nasty

BY JIM ERSKINE AND GEORGE MORAN

Clarkson N. Potter, Inc./Publishers NEW YORK

DISTRIBUTED BY CROWN PUBLISHERS, INC.

Printed in the United States of America
Published simultaneously in Canada by
General Publishing Company Limited

Designed by Betty Binns Graphics

Library of Congress Cataloging in Publication Data

Erskine, Jim.
     Throw a tomato.

     1. American wit and humor.   2. American wit and
humor, Pictorial.   I. Moran, George, 1942–
II. Title.
PN6162.E75   741.5'973   79-14209
ISBN 0-517-53865-2

To John, Rachel, and Linda Mae
who are not responsible   **J. E.**

A nice man is a man of nasty ideas.
—JONATHAN SWIFT

Breed rats.

Toss babies.

Threaten bunnies.

Be obnoxious.

Don't clean up after making your
peanut butter and jelly sandwich.

Use all the hot water.

Pour honey in the mailbox.

Litter.

Starch underwear.

Kick the person in front of you.

Blame it on the person behind you.

Carry a pork chop in your pocket for three weeks.

Walk on the table.

Free your spider collection.

Tailgate.

Trip a grandmother.

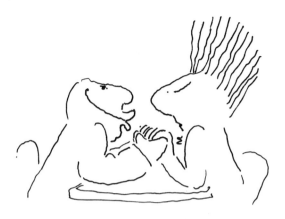

Eat onions.

Don't leave a tip.

Stick out your tongue.

Scratch someone's favorite record.

Spread vicious rumors.

Snore in church.

Burp.

Butter the floor.

Stand in front of the TV.

Rake the leaves into your
neighbor's yard.

Shout in the library.

Jingle your change.

Tear pages out of the phone book.

Point at people.

Steal from the collection plate.

Occupy the bathroom for
unreasonable periods of time.

Stick your hand in the clam dip.

Drop your hors d'oeuvre
and grind it into the carpet.

Hard-boil all the eggs.

Throw a tomato.

Honk as soon as the light changes.

Break a heart.

Hum at a concert.

Cut the strings off all the tea bags.

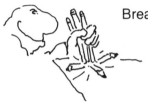

Break all the pencil points. . .

then hide the sharpener.

Don't buy any Christmas presents.

Drive at 25 mph on the freeway.

Unscrew the salt shaker lid.

Jam the pay toilet door.

Don't wipe your feet.

Start a load of washing
as soon as someone gets in the shower.

Forget your mother's birthday.

Crash a funeral.

Giggle during the eulogy.

Pour gravy on your host.

Talk with your mouth full.

Spray-paint someone's eyeglasses.

Say "Huh?" after someone
has spoken to you.

Eat sloppily.

Gloat when you win.

Throw a tantrum when you lose.

Clip your toenails in public.

Go wild with shaving cream.

Leave the cap off the toothpaste.

Soap windows.

Go "a-bugga-bugga-boo"
in people's faces.

Scratch a lot.

Step on some feet.

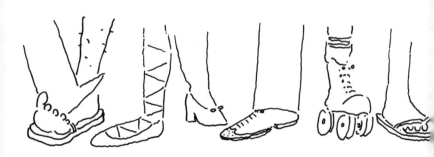

Write insincere love letters.

Never remember anyone's name.

Practice *Chopsticks* with
the windows open.

Leave a cow on your neighbor's porch.

Burn the toast.

Short-sheet the bed.

Go to a party with the measles.

Hide in a dark corner while wearing
an ape mask.

Give inaccurate directions to motorists.

Scream in the dentist's office.

Say "I can do that better than you."

Sit in front of a short person
at the theater.

Go to the hospital and laugh at the patients.

Let your shirttail hang out.

Throw water bombs.

Take up two parking places.

Be unreasonable.

Hoard overdue library books.

Clog the sink.

Cough all through the movie.

Stare at somebody.

Cut the clothesline.

Put your sneakers
in the refrigerator.

Turn up the stereo as loud as possible.

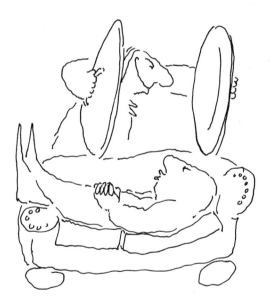

Wake someone up violently.

Tickle people with a branch of poison ivy.

Bite people.

Feign serious illness.

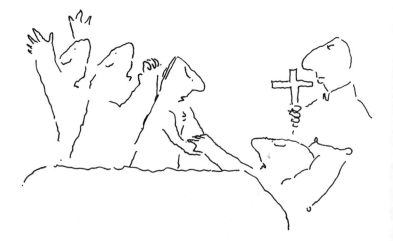

Salt the Band-Aids.

Hide a frog under the pillow.

Stomp through the flower bed.

Enroll your friends in record clubs.

Pull wings off flies.

Use all the toilet paper.

Deny a friend in need.

Harass pedestrians.

Plant ragweed.

Deliver lectures on abstinence
and temperance.

Go to the grocery and squish the fruits.

Smoke large black cigars.

Turn on the sprinkler at a lawn party.

Kick over garbage cans.

Stray into other people's snapshots.

Tell someone she *really*
should lose a few pounds.

Call somebody up at 3 A.M.

Talk gibberish during a serious
conversation.

Press all the buttons in the elevator.

Ruin the punch line.

Ignore *everybody.*

Break something.

Grab someone's nose and don't let go.

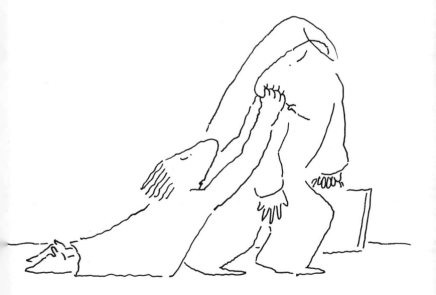

Sneak up on people.

Gnash your teeth.

Make faces at people behind their backs.

Poke people.

Encroach on
someone's turf.

Talk loudly about the person in the next booth at the restaurant.

Throw your chewing gum on the floor.

Take the last cookie.

Put stones in all the shoes.

Don't train your Doberman.

Cheat at MONOPOLY®

Paint your house chartreuse with pink trim.

Leave a ring in the bathtub.

Reveal the ending.

Drop bugs on passersby.

Scream in somebody's ear.

Squirt water through your teeth.

Intimidate somebody.

Saw the leg off a chair.

Don't water the plants.

Demoralize your friends.

Slobber on the couch.

Don't use deodorant.

Snitch.

Snore loudly.

Put gummy stuff inside books.

Scrape your fingernails across the blackboard.

Sing at the dinner table.

Constantly interrupt.

Pour vinegar in the milk.

Lie all the time.

Put piranhas in the swimming pool.

Never say "thank you."